affirmation goddess

express your way
to happiness

Affirmation Goddess: Express Your Way to Happiness
Anita Revel

ISBN 978-0-9804439-8-1

Publisher	Now Age Publishing Pty Ltd PO Box 555, Cowaramup 6284 Western Australia NowAgePublishing.com
Editor	Serene Conneeley :: SereneConneeley.com
Cover design	Inspired Insight :: inspired-insight.com
Cover image	© Patrizia Tilly
Author photograph	Alise Black :: aliseblack.com.au
Card images	Sourced from Fotolia.com

National Library of Australia Cataloguing-in-Publication entry

Author	Revel, Anita, 1968-
Title	Affirmation goddess : express your way to happiness : modern affirmations for modern women / Anita Revel.
ISBN	9780980443981 (pbk.)
Subjects	Affirmations. Self-realization in women. Self-actualization (Psychology) in women. Well-being--Religious aspects. Spiritual life. Happiness. Women--Conduct of life.
Dewey Number	158.1082

affirmation goddess

express your way
to happiness

ANITA REVEL

now age
PUBLISHING

Other Books & Journals by Anita Revel

Sacred Vigilance, Wide-Awake Meditation
(Goddess.com.au, September 2008)

What Would Goddess Do?
A Journal for Channelling Divine Guidance
(Goddess.com.au, March 2009)

BOTIBOTO: Beautiful On The Inside, Beautiful On The Outside, An
Empowerment Story for Well-Rounded Women
(Now Age Publishing eBook April 2009)

The Goddess DIET, See a Goddess in the Mirror in 21 Days
(Now Age Publishing June 2009)

The Goddess Guide to Chakra Vitality, 3rd edition
(Now Age Publishing August 2009)

Goddess Makeover, A Home-study Course in
Personal Values, Self-actualisation and Divine Revellion
(Now Age Publishing March 2010)

Marketing Made Easy for Celebrants,
Boost Your Bookings With Easy and Effective Marketing Methods
(Now Age Publishing June 2010)

7 Day Bootcamp for Brides
Feel Fit, Focused and Fabulous on Your Wedding Day!
(Now Age Publishing July 2010)

table of contents

I crafted this collection of affirmations over many years of practice and action, with modern women in mind. As such, they are linguistically lush, luminous and occasionally a wee bit cheeky.

I trust you will enjoy using them and finding new ways to shine!

Blissed be,
Anita Revel

before you begin

Welcome, beautiful soul. It is no accident that you have found this collection of affirmations and that you are using them now. It is my wish for you that these affirmations will help you manifest your truth – and your heart's desires – through expression and intent.

In my experience, affirmations are one of the most effective "power tools" for intentionally bringing about positive change. With frequent use, you will find yourself stepping into the flow of life easily. You will also notice an increased sense of wellbeing as you progress through affirmations appropriate to your situation.

Thank you for choosing this book! I trust you will enjoy the dozens of affirmations listed within. Before you begin using them, however, allow me to clarify some things…

1. Throughout this book, I speak in the feminine. I simply write this way to avoid the clutter that comes with the he/she/his/her political guff. Spirit does not discriminate; nor is it my intention to do so. For male readers, please interchange the feminine for the masculine as you need to.

2. If using this book as an oracle, understand that the answers that will reveal themselves to you are for

general guidance only. The affirmations are designed to be keys to reveal and manifest your own truth that already exists within you. It is my desire that you use them as tools to connect with your:

- ultimate source of wisdom – your intuition;
- ultimate source of energy – your auric body; and
- ultimate source of inspiration – Spirit.

3. This collection of affirmations is founded on the seven states of wellbeing. There are also some additional "wild cards" to promote holistic wellbeing.

These seven states are interwoven with the chakra system, which it is assumed you already have a working knowledge of. If you need more information I humbly suggest my ever-popular handbook for beginners, *The Goddess Guide to Chakra Vitality*, and the more comprehensive *7-Day Chakra Workout*. A top-line version of the latter is available as a free e-Course at ChakraGoddess.com.

The affirmations and the advice contained herein can be used to guide you, but always consult with your inner knowing, your divine Self, to help you with any life-changing decisions.

the perfect affirmation

By the time you go to bed tonight, you will have had around 60,000 thoughts go through your head. When you reflect on your day, what ratio of your thoughts was positive? Were your thoughts mostly random or deliberate? Out of left-field or in reaction to a catalyst? Using affirmations will help those 60,000 thoughts become 100 percent positive.

An affirmation is a short, positive statement that describes a truth, or an ideal outcome of a wish or desire. Affirmations help maintain a positive mindset and override toxic thinking habits. Instead of listening to shut-down themes of self-criticism, self-doubt and self-loathing, you will begin to see there really is a glimmer of hope for happiness. With practise, the hope becomes your truth.

As well as using affirmations to attract good things, you can also use them to release the effects of negative experiences in your past; to release you from beliefs that life is meant to be hard; and to overcome problems that you simply can't think of rational solutions for.

Your first step to choosing an appropriate affirmation is to identify what you want from your life. Imagine yourself in the situation you desire and describe it in words. By expressing your desire as though it has already come to fruition, you are programming your thoughts and behaviours to manifest the result you are seeking. When you decide "it is to be so" then your intention will literally drive it to be so. It's like reprogramming your thought patterns and habitual behaviour for the power of *good*!

There are three keys to creating an effective affirmation, and three keys to the successful execution of an affirmation.

3 Keys to the Perfect Affirmation

Make it memorable. Keeping your affirmation short and sweet will help you remember it more easily. The better you can remember it, the more likely you will be to use it.

Be positive. Use positive words for positive results. Including negative words in your affirmation only serves to perpetuate the negative energy. For example, if you say, "I am not poor" the mind focuses on "poor" and stays anchored in lack. Self-sabotage occurs as you subconsciously look for opportunities to stay poor. Say instead, "I have plenty of money for all that I need."

Be in the now. Your affirmation must always be written in present tense. Using words like "will do" keeps your outcome in the future, out of your reach. It must also be stated as if your wish has already come true – this helps your brain reprogram your thought patterns to be comfortable and familiar with what your successful situation looks like.

3 Keys to Success

Be dedicated. The affirmation you choose must be a dedicated belief. Your thoughts manifest as you desire, so if your approach is ad hoc – "I'll try it out" – you'll get equally ad hoc results. Using affirmations with your full commitment replaces toxic thinking with positive power.

Believe. Believe with your whole heart that your desire will come true. *Know* that you deserve what you are asking for. When you truly believe, you will receive and achieve.

Persevere. Choose an affirmation and work with it dozens of times daily, seven days a week, every day until your affirmation becomes your reality. It can be spoken out loud, recorded in your private diary repetitively, or written on individual sticky notes and hung around your daily environment. You can even stick your favourite affirmation card on your bathroom mirror, refrigerator or office wall to remind you to focus on your wish all day long.

"We are what we think. And that which we are arises with our thoughts. With our thoughts, we make our world." ~ Buddha

3 Danger Zones – Warning!

When choosing and using affirmations, there are some things to be careful about. They are the misguided goals, the choker and the back-ender.

Misguided Goals

Sometimes when people create their affirmation, they set their sights on something they *think* they need. Such goal-setting can waylay you from focusing on what you *really* need. Who needs an $80,000 car if the repayments are going to restrict your lifestyle? Who needs a five-bedroom mansion when it chews up hours of your time and resources in house-keeping? Who needs a size 0 body when you end up fainting from exhaustion? So, as far as goals are concerned, heed Anthony Robbins and *be careful what you wish for*!

I've learned it doesn't matter what car I drive; it's feeling proud of how I get from Point A to B that's important. It's not a priority how many bedrooms I have; it's enjoying a warm and harmonious home environment that has meaning. And it's not the label on my clothes that counts; it's feeling foxy in them that makes me happy.

So, instead of listing things you'd like to own, simply describe how you'd like to *feel* when you've arrived. Resist being materialistic – *having* a million dollars is not the key to your happiness. *Feeling* like a million dollars is!

The Choker

If you read an affirmation aloud and choke on the words, see this as a sign you have hit the sweet spot of your critic. Go ahead, paint a big red target around this issue and deal with it accordingly. Use the affirmation vigorously until you gradually feel more and more comfortable with your shift.

When you stop choking over your self-validations altogether, congratulations! This means you have harnessed your inner-critic's powers and can now start using them for good. It won't be long before your affirmation comes true!

The Back-Ender

What you hear in your head *after* you've said your affirmation is the real affirmation. For example, what really happens when you look yourself in the eye and say, "I am beautiful"? Is there a whisper of trash-talk? Uh-oh…

If this little voice is laughing, scoffing or challenging your statement, it is overriding your healthy intentions. It is reverting to old habits of self-sabotage. Become aware of nasty whispers such as "This is ridiculous!" or "Oh come on, who in their right mind would really love me?"

Because this negative message is the last thing you hear, this is the message you'll end up acting on! Persevere with training the little critic in your head to work with you rather than against you.

Common Themes for Affirmations

We all want to feel healthy, vibrant and fully alive. But when a pimple appears on our rosy picture, it makes us feel yucky. We want to fix it; to heal it; to get rid of it so we can return to our happy place. Affirmations are useful for seeing the rosy picture rather than the pimple, thereby altering a mindset that is keeping us in a state of non-productiveness.

In all my years of teaching, I have come across literally thousands of pimples that men and women want to "fix". No matter how different they all are though, they can all be condensed down to seven common themes. These themes are encapsulated by the seven states of wellbeing.

If you are feeling stagnant, or feeling lost, or wondering why you keep finding yourself in the same old hurtful situation, for example, focus on affirmations for mental wellbeing – they will relate to clarity, trust and wisdom.

Or if you're feeling fat, frumpy and lethargic, you could focus on affirmations for physical wellbeing. Use words that make you feel strong, purposeful and energetic.

Another example: if you're being bullied at work, use affirmations for your personal wellbeing. Reclaim your boundaries and therefore your personal power.

the seven states of wellbeing

The seven states of wellbeing are the physical, transitional, personal, emotional, creative, mental and spiritual conditions that affect our holistic wellbeing. They can be defined in short as:

▸ **Physical Wellbeing**: The feeling of being strong, balanced, nurtured, fit and vibrant. A physically well person celebrates her physical body and her connection to Earth, family and humanity. She feels grounded, content and comfortable on her chosen path.

▸ **Transitional Wellbeing**: The ability to cope with change and evolution, and to easily "go with the flow" of life. A person in a state of transitional wellness is comfortable with infinite abundance, her feminine divine, emotional and Universal flow, the sacred balance of yin and yang, and creative freedom through flexibility and adaptation.

▸ **Personal Wellbeing**: The state of having clear boundaries and a solid understanding of Self. A robust personality is proud of her Self and her actions in all her aspects – light and shadow, public and private, loud and soft, young and old, and so on. She has a healthy sense of identity and upholds her values easily.

- **Emotional Wellbeing**: An ability to be open to relationships based on mutual respect, truth, warmth and admiration. An emotionally well person fosters mutually fulfilling relationships at all levels – professional, personal, intimate, familial and social. She operates from a space of love at all levels – knowing, thinking, doing, being.

- **Creative Wellbeing**: The state of being able to express oneself clearly and creatively, free from conditioning and fear. A creative person speaks her truth with diplomacy and shares her learnings with grace. When she speaks, she is heard. Just as easily, when others speak, she listens. She is a natural healer in her community, respected for her precise, astute, creative and relevant contributions.

- **Mental Wellbeing**: The state of being free of toxicity and having trust in one's own wisdom and capability. A mentally astute person clearly knows what is right for her as well as her wider community, and acts in accordance with her innate wisdom and intuition.

- **Spiritual Wellbeing**: The ability to find bliss in connection with the divine; with the essence that makes joy possible. A spiritually well person revels in her divine purpose/work with gratitude, dignity and joy. She sleeps easily, has happy dreams, and smiles often.

how to use this book

This book depicts beautiful images that make up a deck of affirmation cards. These cards are available from AffirmationGoddess.com. Even if you don't have the cards, however, you can still use this book in many useful ways.

As an Oracle

An oracle is a divination tool that helps reveal answers or show you ways to move forward. Use this book as an oracle by opening it at random on a page with an image and interpretation. Use the affirmation that resonates with you the strongest throughout your day or week. In using it, a deep issue you were previously unaware of may very well surface for healing and transformation.

As a Guide to Problem Solving

As I touched on earlier, sometimes we have the rosiest of lives but for a "pimple" on the scene. If you know what the problem is, you can go directly to the section that will help you best deal with it. For example, if you are lacking in energy or oomph, go to the Affirmations for Physical Wellbeing section to become fitter, more grounded and/or more comfortable with your direction.

If you don't know what the bug-bear is, however, you can either use the book as an oracle, as described previously, or use your preferred chakra-healing method to determine which of your chakras is blocked. Once you know where you are blocked, and therefore which state of wellbeing needs addressing, use an appropriate affirmation to clear the blockage.

The states of wellbeing and their associated chakras are:

- Physical wellbeing: Base chakra
- Transitional wellbeing: Sacral chakra
- Personal wellbeing: Solar Plexus chakra
- Emotional wellbeing: Heart chakra
- Creative wellbeing: Throat chakra
- Mental wellbeing: Third-eye chakra
- Spiritual wellbeing: Crown chakra
- Holistic wellbeing: All chakras in balance at once

As Inspiration

Occasionally you will come across an image or affirmation that just sings to you. You'll want to cut it out and keep it in your wallet, in your journal or in your office. Rather than damaging your book, permission is granted to photocopy up to five percent of this book for personal use. This means you may copy up to seven pages to stick on your mirror or pin-up board. (After that, copyright law kicks in and you may not take copies without further permission. Contact the publisher for details.) Use the image as inspiration to stick with your affirmation until you manifest your desire.

Using The Affirmation Cards

The affirmation cards depicted in this book are very user-friendly – you can use them in many ways to achieve the results you're seeking. Here are just some ideas for how you can use them:

- Flick through the deck and write down your very first reaction upon seeing each card. When you find one that resonates, work with the affirmation or theme until you get a result. Inverse meanings are also suggested in this guide, so if you have an adverse reaction to a card, work to eliminate the negative energy.

- Create rapport with your cards. Spend time gazing at the pictures and holding the cards to your heart. This guide does offer expanded card meanings, but remain open to additional messages revealed to you via each card.

- Pull a single card each day to answer a question, to confirm what you already know is true, or as a mini-reading. If it's a reading, shuffle the cards and ask, "What do I need to know today?" Journal how the message applies to your situation, and act according to how your card and intuition guide you.

- Healers, therapists and yoga instructors may use the cards to identify blockages in their clients. Individuals can do the same for themselves. If you "choke" on an affirmation, work with it to identify issues that need resolving or healing. For example, if you pull a card relating to personal boundaries, look for signs of manipulation, abuse, disrespect, causes of anxiety, or events that disconnect you from your authentic Self. Then, examine ways to resolve this blockage. You may choose to work with the affirmation provided with that card, or choose another affirmation to resolve the situation.

Ideas For Layouts

You might also choose to lay out your cards in your favourite style. Here are some ideas to start with:

- **Simple One-Card Layout**: Ensure you get a good answer by asking a good question! Make sure it applies to you and your situation, and includes a request for guidance. For example, *What is this situation teaching me? What lesson have I yet to learn?* Or even, *How can I achieve…?*

- **Basic Three-Card Layout** The first card focuses on your past, the second on your present and the third on your future.

- **Triple Feminine Healing**: Focus on your maiden, matron, maven aspects – your conditioning from childhood; major influences as you've grown into adulthood; and where your strengths and gifts lie as a wise woman and teacher. For men, work with the warrior, father, sage aspects.

the affirmations...

One hug for friendship,
two for love; tree hugs for me
and my family

affirmation goddess

Anita Revel

affirmations for physical wellbeing

Be Present

Physical wellbeing forms your foundation. When you are in tune physically, you are able to connect with humanity, your purpose, and that which makes you feel secure. When you are connected with the life-force of Mother Earth, you can experience a dynamic presence – you are visible, you are valuable, you are safe, and you matter. As a physically well person you can develop passion for your purpose, feel like a valued member of your communities, and be fulfilled by the path that reveals itself to you. You can also experience and relish what it is to *be present*.

When you are present you can:

▸ Celebrate your physical body.
▸ Carve your own path and lead by example.
▸ Respond to threats and chaos with rationality and calm.
▸ Be deeply connected with Mother Earth and humanity.
▸ Consider yourself a valuable member of the community.
▸ Uphold the traditions of your human tribe – your ancestors, friends and community.

Life: dish it up baby, and
don't be stingy with the jalapeños

affirmation goddess

Anita Revel

Passion / Apathy

Every great venture has been fuelled by passion. A project can't come to fruition without your enthusiasm and willingness to act on your vision. This is your passion in action.

Passion is "working" to ensure the future of your life, a person or a project, but it's not hard or difficult work. Rather, it's a fun and satisfying pursuit. Having passion means you are able to become emotional about your existence and you can revisit the enthusiasm for life you enjoyed as a child. Work becomes play, and play is joyous and easy.

If you're feeling apathetic about the project, it's time to either let the project go, or find a new angle that will stir your passion for its success.

Also be aware that it is difficult to be apathetic when you are proud to be with the person you're alone with! So, turn on the light you are capable of shining, and radiate your passion with ease.

I am safe;
my friends have my back

affirmation goddess

Anita Revel

Community / Isolation

~ I am recognised for my contributions.
~ I am a valuable member of my community.
~ My community serves me as well as I serve it.

The first community you knew was your family. As you grew up you entered a playgroup, then school, then sporting teams and your immediate neighbourhood. You launched into adulthood and gravitated to social, work or more global communities – groups of like-minded people with aligned passions and ideals. Even online, communities exist to achieve a greater cause: meaningful connections with others that validate your thoughts, ethics and be-ing.

As such, being part of a community is a primal urge instilled from birth. If you were over-protected, isolated or abused as a youngster, you'll need to repair the isolation instilled in your formative years.

Foster bonds with your community. Meet your neighbours, smile at people in your street, get involved in local events, coach a sports team, volunteer locally, start a common interest group and share your resources. Getting involved helps to alleviate feelings of isolation.

Each time I believe
I am making a difference, I am

affirmation goddess

Anita Revel

Security / Vulnerability

~ Real security comes from within.

~ My feet are firmly planted; I am at home.

~ The Universe provides plenty of what I need.

In 1943, psychologist Abraham Maslow theorised that humans focus on desires according to a hierarchy of needs. The first level describes the most fundamental needs. Being grounded and secure is the second-most fundamental need, and one which must be mastered before we can focus on the higher needs of love, esteem and self-actualisation.

Your sense of security comes under threat when events beyond your control sends you into a spiral – death, divorce, a child leaving home, a major illness, loss of a job or a best friend leaving town. Even an electrical blackout or water shortage can throw you off balance.

See any state of chaos as an opportunity to release your attachment to how you think things *should* be. Reassess the value you place on your own skills and worth – chances are you're selling yourself short. Also know that security does not depend purely on outer circumstances; it comes from your realisation that you are loved, wanted and valued.

I am living my life
forwards

affirmation goddess

Anita Revel

Life Direction / Lack of Purpose

~ My purpose is obvious when my values align.

~ My path reveals itself to me easily and naturally.

~ I am grateful for the signs that guide me on my journey.

How do you answer when asked, "What do you do?" Do you pigeon-hole yourself as a cop, nurse, teacher, builder, prime minister or "just" a mum? Or you describe your passions, ambitions and values?

Having a satisfying career or parental vocation is a worthy dream, yet what really matters are your values as you carry out your role. Begin by listing the values you hold sacred, then see your life direction magically unfold before you as your principles come into alignment with your purpose.

See yourself setting off down the *high*way of life (*high*, as in noble; the right way), and trust that your willingness to bide by your values will keep you on the straight and narrow for your highest good.

It's not necessary to search deeply for the meaning of life; simply trust that this process will manifest your heart and soul's true desires.

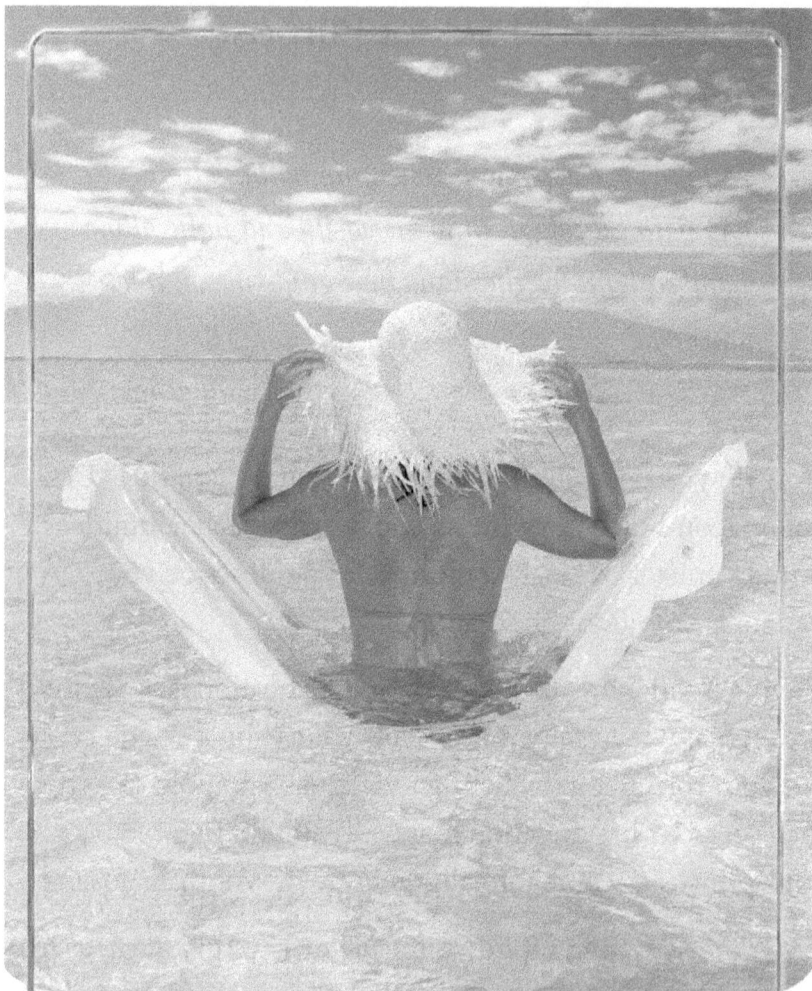

Though storms may rise and
rock my boat, I'm grateful for lessons
that keep me afloat

affirmation goddess

Anita Revel

Grounded / Adrift

~ Every cell of my body stems from Mother Earth.
~ I have common ground with every living organism.
~ I am as old and as young, as wise and as innocent,
  as complex and as simple as Mother Earth herself.

The ancient Romans believed every element in the Universe, whether on land, in the sea or in the sky, was a single living entity of Gaia, the primordial Great Mother. Like any mother, she is the source of life and inherent wisdom, and provides your basic needs.

No matter where you live or travel, no matter what you eat or how you pray, no matter who you marry or where you grew up, Gaia's love and sustenance is the one thing we all have in common. She is the Great Mother who connects us all, making us citizens of her one global village.

When you can feel her pulse, her living vibration, you are connected to the ultimate life-source. Just as a tree's roots furrow into the ground to flourish, imagine yourself deeply rooted to Gaia to flourish also. Feel yourself become grounded and physically robust. You cannot lose your way when you are connected to such beautiful mother love.

Friends are but
an arm's reach away

affirmation goddess

Anita Revel

Humanity / Detachment

~ I am a valuable member of Gaia's global village.
~ I am a bridge-builder in the matrix of humanity.
~ The divine light in all human beings uplifts me.

According to the United States Census Bureau, there are more than 6.773 billion people in the world. While it's impossible to know each individual personally, it is possible to recognise a common human trait amongst us all: we love.

We share our hearts, celebrate our joys and delight in the presence of others. We also hurt, we worry, and we feel isolated if we don't belong to a tribe. When we feel that we don't belong, loneliness, stagnancy and detachment ensues.

If any of these words describe you, reassess your role in your community and identify where you fit in. Whether you're the soccer coach, the mayor or the hermit artist, the role you play is a vital ingredient in the whole pie of humanity.

Detachment persists if you blame an unfair world or cruel circumstances for your problems. As the saying goes, *build a bridge and get over it*. Use the bridge to reattach yourself to humanity. Return to the heart-space that connects all global citizens and focus on the bridges, not the walls.

The best way to be a sex object
is to object to meaningless sex

affirmation goddess

Anita Revel

Sexuality / Prudishness

~ The light of my feminine divine is turned ON.

~ I am the sexiest thing that has ever happened to me.

~ My divine essence is expressed via my physical Self.

According to myth, the Greek goddess Aphrodite emerged as a nymph from the ocean and drove almost every male god wild with desire. The light of her feminine divine was definitely turned *on*.

Sadly, for many men and women it is not so easy to express the divine essence through the physical Self. Perhaps there's an unresolved issue related to your body image, feelings of shame or an emotional blockage preventing intimacy, or maybe you've not been taught the art of sexual expression.

Given that sex is such a vital ingredient in many romantic relationships, direct your energy towards becoming a magnet for a physically satisfying connection with your partner. Consciously loosen your limbs, open your heart, and see yourself as a juicy, playful, sexy being.

Regardless of your shape or size, embracing your sexuality will help you escape the loop of self-loathing. When your divine spark is free to shine, you will bedazzle.

Everybody is beautiful,
at every age and every stage

affirmation goddess

Anita Revel

affirmations for transitional wellbeing

Feel the Flow

When you are comfortable with change, you avail yourself to new opportunities. You become open to more time, energy, creativity, resources and love. This requires you to step into the Universal current; to allow time for introspection, relaxation and observation. Doing this makes you more receptive to the flow of life. You can release attachment to expectations, take it easy during transitions, open yourself to all possibilities, allow emotions to run their course, and ignite the divine spark that resides within.

When you can step into the flow of the Universe you can:

▸ Relish beauty and embody grace.
▸ Accept and manage change gracefully.
▸ Attract abundance which is exactly right for you.
▸ Openly release any need to control external forces.
▸ Love your essence, both physically and spiritually.
▸ "Go with the flow" whilst maintaining your purpose.
▸ Nourish yourself with enough sleep, good food, fresh air and time for your passions and hobbies.

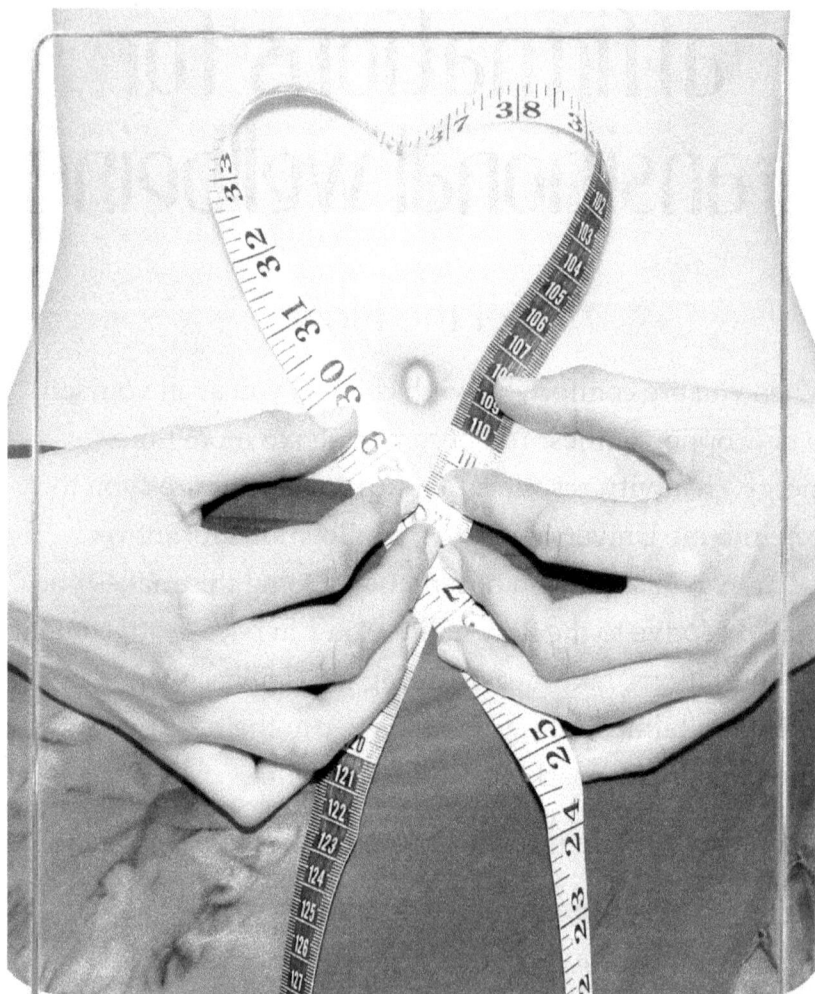

I am fit, focused
and fabulous

affirmation goddess

Anita Revel

Nourishment / Abuse

> ~ *I am fit, fluid and fabulous.*
>
> ~ *I relish food, fitness, recreation and rest.*
>
> ~ *The more I move, the more energy I have.*

The funny thing about the body is that unless it complains, we tend to take it for granted – but in taking it for granted we give it cause to complain! The body is our vehicle for life, and just like a car it is important to keep it tuned.

Its needs are quite simple, relying on just four elements for health. Supply it with good food, water, enjoyable exercise and rest, and enjoy a return to good health. See these four elements as nourishment for your body rather than tools to fulfil an emotional hunger. Balance your food and fitness, recreation and rest, and your body will be good for miles and miles and miles.

Also heed the wisdom in The Desiderata of Happiness (Latin for "desired things"– the inspirational poem about attaining happiness in life):

Take kindly the counsel of the years, gracefully surrendering the things of youth.

Every choice I make
is the right one

affirmation goddess

Anita Revel

Change / Inertia

~ *Onwards I flow, upwards I grow.*
~ *Youthful beauty fades; sassy is forever.*
~ *Change is healthy – it keeps me on the move.*

Change is inevitable (except from a vending machine). Everything around you and within you changes – it evolves, progresses, regresses, morphs and transforms. It is only when you resist change that it becomes a problem.

It's natural to want to stand your ground and wrap yourself in all that is familiar, but remember: change brings with it new opportunities, creative energy and a fresh outlook.

The only reason to be afraid of change is if you think things are going to get worse, yet resisting change keeps you in a state of inertia rather than growth.

Move beyond the denial and resistance, and get excited about exploring new options. Admit some change is beyond your control and anticipate how things can only get better.

When you are ready to commit to improving your circumstances through change, get ready to take your life onwards and upwards!

My creative spark is
switched ON

affirmation goddess

Anita Revel

Wild Woman / Control Freak

~ I am naturally wild and free.
~ My creativity flows with wild abandon.
~ I embrace more fun, more happiness, more meaning.

Does your inner wild woman have a name? Are you aware that she resides within? Do you know what it is that she yearns for the most? Or are you too busy controlling your life and the outcomes of your decisions?

Control shuts down your sacral chakra, your home of fluidity and fun. Control keeps you trapped in a small box of expectations and daily routine.

Relinquish control by connecting with your wild woman. Experience unbridled freedom and abundant blissings. Look within and identify that primal craving for more – more fun, more happiness, more meaning.

Your wild woman is a glowing ember of hope. Can you see her? Name her! Unfurl her longings and throw her deepest desires to the wind. Sit by a river and release controlling habits to the water's flow. See how easy it is to surrender your grip and watch your worries float away!

When I shimmy and shake,
shimmer and shine,
I engage my feminine divine

affirmation goddess

Anita Revel

Divine Self / Self-Loathing

~ I am real-ly beauty-full.

~ I am vibing magnificence!

~ I am awakening to the beautiful Self I really am.

If you're the type to look in the mirror and criticise yourself day after day, you are in a self-loathing loop. Beginning the day with criticism sets you on a course of destruction for the next 24 hours. You'll eat in excess because you're "fat and ugly anyway." You'll avoid exercise because "what's the point?" In effect, you will manifest a "fat and ugly" body because that's the intention you set from your first waking moment.

Turn your thoughts instead to self-appreciation. Look your reflection in the eye and say, "Good morning beautiful!"

While you're appreciating your reflection, notice your perfections. Affirm your uniqueness. Treasure the gifts that you have to offer. Embrace your sacred potential. Radiate the Divine Self that resides within. Vibe magnificence. Stretch gently and magically. Say, "My bum looks great in this!" Promise yourself the best of everything today. Awaken to the beauty in and around you to attract more of the same.

I am surrounded by love,
as below so above

affirmation goddess

Abundance / Poverty

~ I am living abundantly.
~ I have all that I need, when I need it.
~ I have an abundance of time, money and love.

Poverty consciousness is a state of mind and heart whereby your values are aligned with material lack.

It may not be obvious if you're under the spell of poverty consciousness, but some good clues are: you often say, "I don't have..."; you refuse to charge full price for your services; or you feel that you're always playing catch-up with your bills.

These values may stem from childhood hardships, a lack of self-worth, or skewed beliefs about what success looks like.

Change your vernacular to begin sentences with "I have plenty..." and begin your list of what it is you have plenty of – money, time, knowledge, skills, support, energy, health, passion...

Start a new relationship with money and see it as a form of energy that exists simply and solely to be exchanged for blessings to keep you safe, well and happy.

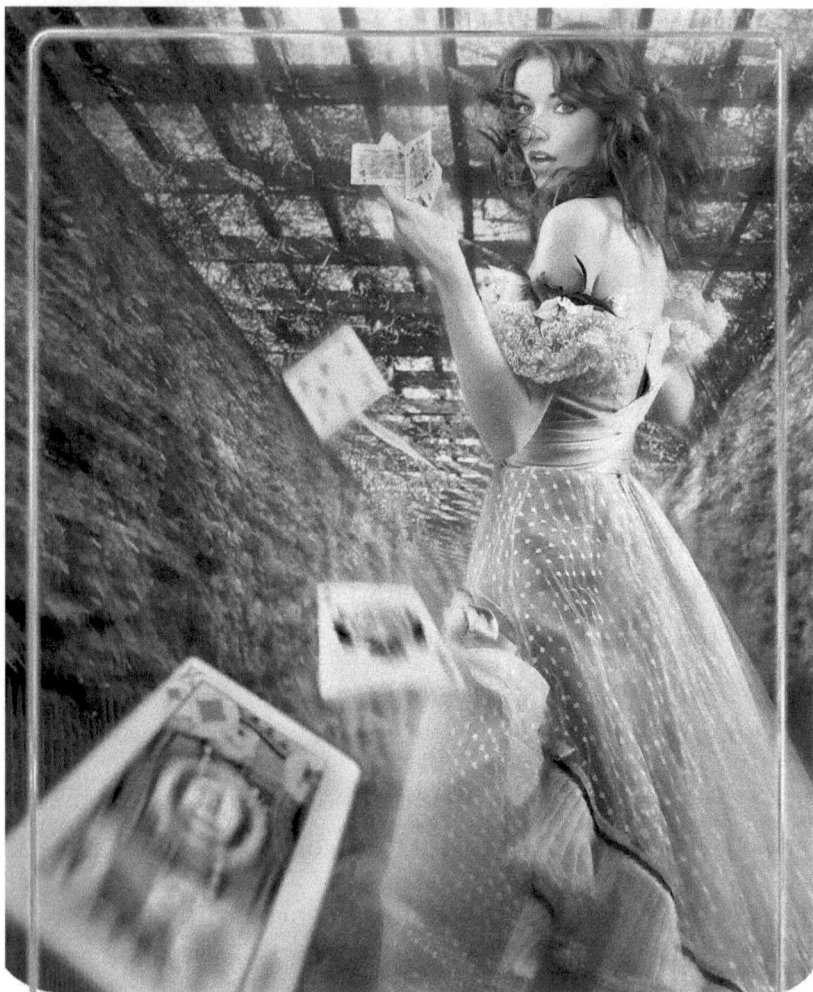

I am fully available
to be struck by luck

affirmation goddess

Anita Revel

Luck / Loss

~ I am a lucky ducky!
~ I am rewarded for good work with good fortune.
~ I expect luck, I deserve luck and I appreciate luck.

Good luck is something millions of people wish for every day, yet few have mastered the art of receiving it. The underlying essence of *getting* lucky is basically believing that you *are* lucky.

If luck is something that happens to other people, check your attitude. Do you think in terms of lack and loss? Change your thinking, actions and words to align with abundance. See yourself as a worthy recipient of the resulting luck when you become available to it.

US president and author of the Declaration of Independence Thomas Jefferson said of luck, "I'm a great believer in luck, and I find the harder I work, the more I have of it." He didn't sit around and wait for it. To be struck by luck, therefore, requires that you expect it, you deserve it, and you are willing to work for it.

To attract luck, act on your hunches, vibe success, notice opportunities and most importantly, take them up.

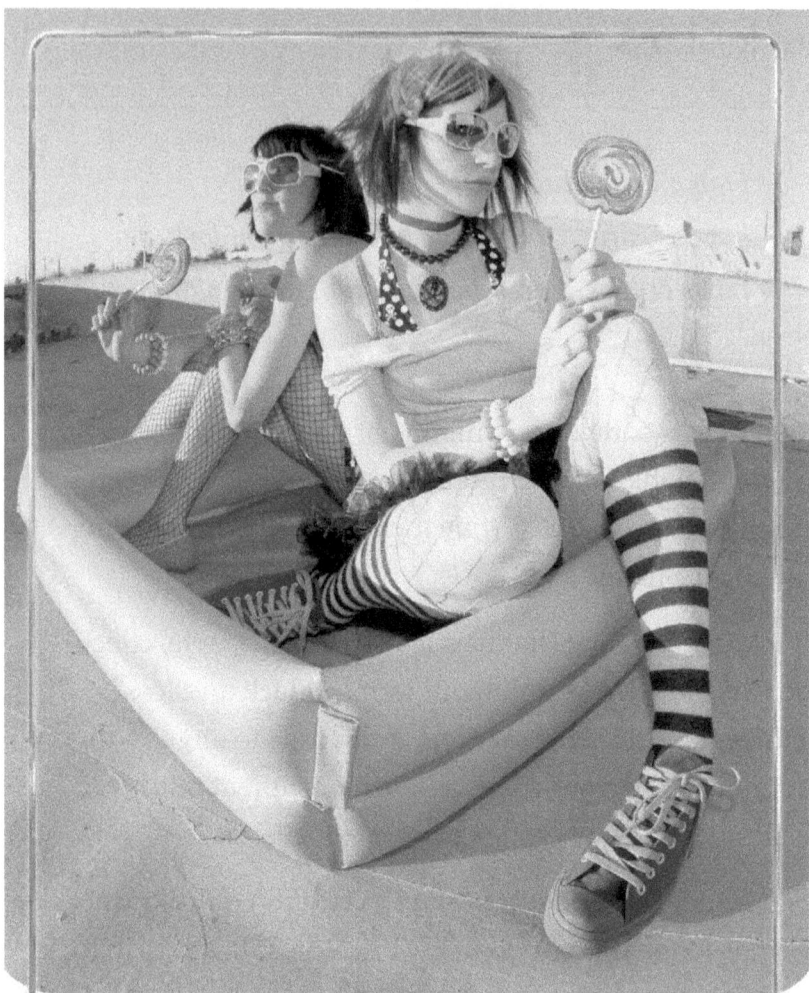

Today's adventures
are tomorrow's morning tea

affirmation goddess

Anita Revel

Spontaneity / Rigidity

~ Hi ho, hi ho, who knows where I will go?
~ Where the wind blows is where my heart goes.
~ My days are filled with laughter and spontaneity.

Are you stuck doing the same thing day in, day out? If so, ask yourself, "When's the last time I did something spontaneous?" If you can't even recall the last time, maybe – just maybe – you're in the danger zone of being a rigid bore. Could this be true of you?

Take baby steps to knock down the walls of rigidity. Unleash your heart's true expression by giving it room to fly. Begin by laughing more each day, especially when you feel yourself slip into the auto-pilot routine.

Laughter is the Universal language of joy. It is your body's way of releasing anxiety, fear and stress and replacing them with feel-good hormones. It is the state of eustress – the good stress – and promotes healthy and positive emotions.

Life's problems become trivial in the light of a good laugh. So actively seek external triggers to help you start laughing! If all else fails, fake it. Chuckle, chortle, giggle, snort or guffaw, and let the infectious nature of laughter take over.

I am free to be,
free to be me

affirmation goddess

Anita Revel

affirmations for personal wellbeing

Know Thyself

Herein dwells the authentic Self; the truth of who you really are. Herein lives the source of your inner wisdom – your intuition. And herein is the Source of your personal power, your map and identity, and where you define and defend your boundaries. Personal wellbeing is your divine essence, which makes you unique, strong and impeccably authentic in your chosen roles. It allows you to accept that patience is both a lesson and a gift; you can relax knowing that you have time, courage and validity on your side.

When you know who you truly are, you can:

▸ Live, breathe and present your authentic Self.
▸ Be intrinsically connected to your intuitive Self.
▸ Accept the consequences of your choices, good and bad.
▸ Understand you are responsible for how you treat others.
▸ Know that anxiety and "butterflies" are really your inner tigress preparing you for success.
▸ Allow your inner wisdom to guide your decision-making and actions.

I am the best thing
that has ever happened to me

affirmation goddess

Anita Revel

Boundaries / Exploitation

~ Respect begets respect.
~ I am my own tigress mother.
~ My boundaries are clear and keep me safe.

Sometimes you may find yourself modifying your behaviour to suit others. Some compromise is fine, but if you're denying your true needs simply to avoid rejection or to keep the peace, you are sending the message that your needs aren't worthy of acknowledgement; that your boundaries are wishy-washy and can be trampled on at will.

Setting boundaries shows others how they can or cannot treat you. It also gives them permission to treat you with the respect you deserve. In order to make boundaries effective, imagine drawing a line in the sand and defining what kind of behaviour is acceptable on one side of that line, and what kind is unacceptable on the other side. Next, decide on suitable consequences in response to exploitive behaviour and conduct that "crosses the line". A consequence is not a punishment or a threat but a statement of what you will do if such behaviour continues. Be prepared to carry out the consequence in order to restore your power.

The time has come to
step up and shine

affirmation goddess

Anita Revel

Individuality / Conformity

~ I cherish forever what makes me unique.
~ I am the fish that swims against the stream.
~ I am a star, born to shine, in my own unique way,
in my own sweet time.

It is traditional for us to wish on the first star we see each evening, but isn't it wonderful to gaze upon the cascade of stars that follow too?

Each and every star is as unique and magnificent to look upon as its neighbour, yet part of the beauty of individuality is being able to delight in the diversity of others also.

Each star plays its own role as part of the big picture, whilst maintaining its own integral position in the Universe.

The same principle applies to you. Biochemically speaking, you are different from every other person who ever was or ever will be. You are as unique as your finger-prints, in your personality, appearance, likes and dislikes.

So be the splash of colour that brightens a monochrome landscape. Like Bette Midler said, "Cherish forever what makes you unique, 'cuz you're really a yawn if it goes!"

I can be the candle that burns
or the match that ignites it

affirmation goddess

Anita Revel

Confidence / Manipulation

~ I am a confident, radiant being.

~ What's the best that can happen?

~ When I get to the edge I intuitively fly.

Confidence is maintaining an expectation for a positive outcome. Allowing negative thoughts, people or experiences to creep in undermines your right to happiness.

Your confidence is low when you feel "butterflies" in your gut. This is your fight or flight mechanism kicking in to protect you from harm. Perhaps someone is manipulating you with bullying tactics, or deflecting their fears or guilt onto you. It could be you're on edge waiting for the worst to happen because, well, you have a habit of asking, "What's the worst that can happen?" Or maybe a bad experience has made you gun-shy of what could happen next.

See these shackles for what they really are – confidence under-miners. Tell them to go away – they are not welcome!

Be persistent in your goal for empowerment and reclaim your right to make your own choices, to be your own Self, and to expect the best. In short, be yourself – as the saying goes, *there's no-one better qualified.*

Removing my mask
reveals the divine

affirmation goddess

Anita Revel

Authenticity / Façade

~ *I am as beautiful within as I am without.*
~ *My authentic Self leads me to my authentic path.*
~ *It is a relief to drop pretence and embrace reality.*

Every person is said to have at least two selves – one without any guise and the other, that which you present to the world. Presenting a polite, valiant, socially-astute Self to the world can be described metaphorically as "wearing a mask". Masks are empowering in that they let you shape-shift into something other than yourself. You can use your mask as a conduit to channel power, magic and mystery that you may not have had the courage to do otherwise. Yet while masks let you tap into your divine essence, without care they can become a crutch – over-reliance on your mask can conceal the human, authentic Self within.

It is this Self behind the mask that holds the key to joy-ever-after. Herein is the home of your deepest desires, your true path, your genuine truth. Drop the mask to tap into this powerful energy – your true divine – and live more authent-ically than ever before. Become *real* to be *real*ly beautiful, and to *real*ise the worth of your Self and your true purpose.

Life may not be the party
I hoped for, but while I'm here,
I'm gonna dance

affirmation goddess

Anita Revel

Optimism / Defeatism

~ *I am an optimistic fatalist.*

~ *I'm a "fantastic enthusiastic".*

~ *Each time I believe I am making a difference, I am.*

The word enthusiasm comes from *en thuse* meaning "in Zeus". Thus, when you face the world with enthusiasm you are doing so charged with the power of the gods.

When you exude the vitality of such divinity, you glow with inner health and wellbeing. To rouse enthusiasm, it's important to be optimistic. This allows you to override any disempowering beliefs based in fatalism. The apparent constraints of fate don't apply when you are optimistic. When you are confident of a positive result, you can reclaim your power over the vagaries of fate and leave behind any lingering sense of doom.

Take steps to restructure and formulate your destiny. Instead of saying, "It's fate that I'm not in a relationship," be an optimistic fatalist and put yourself in the position to be kissed. Be positively loud and firm as you say, "I am fated for wonderful relationships!" Make yourself available to good results and enjoy your luck as it comes rolling in.

Today I realise...
I have been perfect all along

affirmation goddess

Anita Revel

Authority / Submission

> ~ *To thine owned Self I am true.*
> ~ *My external life supports my inner values.*
> ~ *I reclaim my power, easily and with integrity!*

Take heed of the wise words of US First Lady, writer and social activist Eleanor Roosevelt: *Nobody can make you feel inferior without your permission.*

In understanding this concept, begin to see that authorities, institutions and even other people only have dominance over you when you acknowledge them to have such control.

In placing your trust in external forces such as banks, government and god, you are living an external life – your attention is on the pursuit of values outside of our own. Too much reliance on such external forces distracts you from your true purpose, your sense of being and your unique Self.

Reclaim your power. You can now rely on yourself for your personal wellbeing. Introduce the word *inner-* to your vernacular, and have fun meeting your inner-child, inner-goddess, inner-star, inner-wow factor… Own who you are, and to thine *owned* self be true – you have been perfect all along, after all.

If love is an ocean,
let me fall in

affirmation goddess

Anita Revel

Courage / Lost Opportunity

> ~ *I am grace under fire.*
> ~ *The best time to start living, is now.*
> ~ *When opportunity knocks, I answer the door.*

Courage is about choosing the right course regardless of the fear factor. It's more than being brave; courage is acting from the heart – doing what's right rather than what's convenient, easy or expected.

You are being courageous when you follow your heart and your intuition. You'll know if courage is required if you feel your heart thumping as if it wants to jump out of your chest. This is your heart's desire in action – "Take action!" it sings. It will also feel heavy if you are ruing lost opportunities, or wishing you had done more with your life by now.

Nobel Prize winning author Ernest Hemingway said, "Courage is grace under fire." Embody grace as you rally your courage. Name the fear that is holding you back and forge forward. Switch off the auto-pilot and reclaim the dream. Release the wisps of lost dreams and choose grace and courage instead. Resolve to do and be your best, and *voila*, it is so.

Blissings shower themselves
upon me

affirmation goddess

Anita Revel

affirmations for emotional wellbeing

Love Fearlessly

When you are in a healthy emotional state, you are able to love deeply, feel compassion, be empathetic and enjoy a deep sense of peace and harmony. It allows you to make meaningful connections with others so that intimacy, trust and self-respect are easy states to achieve. Openness, self-appreciation and benevolence are values that naturally become sacred, enabling you to receive as much respect and love as you are willing and able to give.

When you are loving fearlessly you can:

▸ Think love; be love.
▸ Embody love, compassion and trust.
▸ Never, ever accept or settle for second best.
▸ Break down walls made of fear, guilt and mistrust.
▸ Invite in joy, reciprocated love and uplifting light.
▸ Happily give these gifts to others and receive them back.
▸ Revel in your self-respect, self-love and self-appreciation.
▸ Behave in accordance with the Three G-forces of Love: Grace, Generosity and Gratitude.

Gratitude is the mother of
happiness; Grace and
Generosity its sisters

affirmation goddess

Anita Revel

Love / Fear

~ Be love, be loved.

~ I am loved as much as I love.

~ The key to joy lies within my capacity for Self love.

There are two main forces in the Universe that influence decision-making and values: love and fear. You have the choice to act from either space.

When you hold the scales of justice in your hand you can see what can be gained with love on one side (the Three G-forces of Love: Gratitude, Grace and Generosity), and what can be lost with fear on the other side (the Three Heartbreak-Rs: Regrets, Reproach and Retribution).

So much is gained when you act from a space of love: balance, healing, meaningful connections, self-appreciation, trust, forgiveness, gratitude and joy.

If your scales ever tip towards fear, consciously step into a space of love, and act knowing you are supported by the Universe's greatest power. This can be done by first aligning your thoughts with the vibration you seek to attract: I *love* love! I *choose* love! I *think* love! I *am* love! Be love, be loved.

I am a reflection of
the love in my life

affirmation goddess

Anita Revel

Generosity / Greed

~ The more I give the more I receive.
~ I have infinite abundance to spend and share.
~ I act in accordance with the Law of Benevolence.

The Universal Law of Three-Fold Return means the more you give away, the more that comes back to you. It sounds good in theory, but there is a catch… you can't give something away with the motivation that it's scoring you karmic points.

When you give your time, energy or material items, you must release any ulterior motives for personal gain; your gift must come from a place of true benevolence. After all, generosity is about sharing resources for the greatest good of all – to think otherwise is a self-centred act of greed and is bound to backfire.

Practise the Law of Benevolence – it's like the Law of Attraction only you're acting as a proxy for other people and asking the Universe for blessings on their behalf.

Once you have mastered the art of giving you will find it a thousand-fold easier to accept help, compliments and good wishes in return.

As I honour my world,
I honour myself

affirmation goddess

Anita Revel

Honour / Guilt

~ Values that I hold sacred are ...
~ I act in accordance with my beliefs.
~ I believe in my honourable and beautiful Self.

Guilt is generally considered an undesirable emotion, but it isn't *all* bad – after all, it is the discomfort you feel when you go against your own conscience, and as such, keeps you honest to your Self.

But if you refuse to change even though you know better, you create a short-cut to self-sabotage. Wallowing in guilt, you become untrusting of others, self-deprecating about your success, and expect bad things to happen as payback.

You can alleviate guilt by acting in accordance with your beliefs; by being true to the values you hold most sacred. When you can integrate your values, goals and behaviours, you will be honouring your highest Self to achieve your highest potential.

Start a list and describe what your ideal values, goals and behaviours look like. You know you are honouring your Self when you can say "Yes, I'm doing that," to 100 percent of the items on your list.

Life and love, ebbing and flowing,
ever changing, ever growing

affirmation goddess

Anita Revel

Forgiveness / Resentment

~ I forgive myself.

~ Forgiveness frees up the rent space in my head.

~ Because I have but one life to live, it's in my best interest to let go and forgive.

Just google "forgiveness" and you'll get thousands of resources telling you why it's so important. But it all boils down to one basic point: if you don't forgive, it's like giving someone free rent in your head-space. That person gets free reign to torment you, undermine you and walk all over you.

Forgiveness is often cited as the hardest thing to do, yet it is one of the most essential. It is not something that can be achieved with medicine or a magic pill. It requires a conscious choice to eliminate toxic thoughts, past hurts and your resistance to giving and receiving unconditional love.

Aim to forgive any past transgressions that are eating away at you. Even if you can't forgive a particular situation (yet), forgive your *Self* for holding on to the injury. In other words, forgive yourself for not being able to forgive!

Offer your heart piece by piece until you can forgive the situation as well.

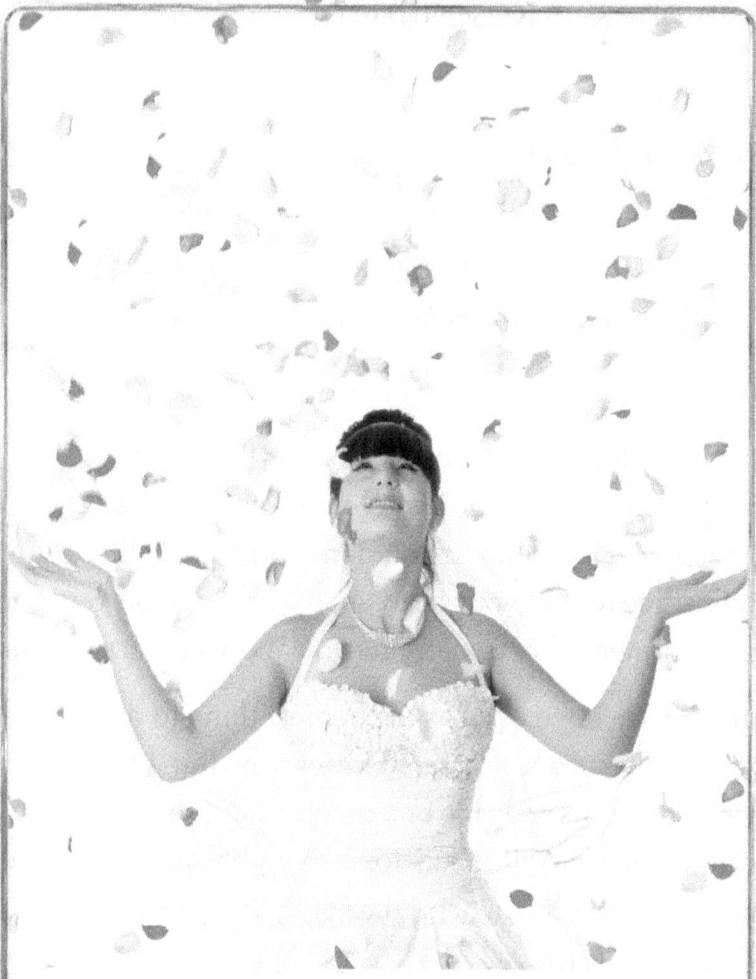

Everything I do today
is an act of self love

affirmation goddess

Anita Revel

Warmth / Coldness

~ It is easy to belong when love is strong.
~ The wider my love, the warmer my heart.
~ Opening to warmth is a choice I willingly make.

Being warm is about being open and willing to share your light, as well as being willing to receive it. A warm person is a magnet for positive energy who attracts loving people with an equal amount of integrity to share.

Opening up may be difficult to begin with, but once you face your past, your fears and your deepest hopes, you can easily glide into the slipstream of the Universe's greatest power: *love.*

In fact, you won't be able to stop yourself from being caught up in the embrace of belonging, of being loved, and of being healed at a very deep level.

Opening to this energy is a choice. You can open your heart to it, keep it protected behind a wall, or choose to open it by small degrees, day by day, step by step. Even if you have been hurt and think it's safer to stay closed, the Universe will always provide you with the love you are open to, in equal measure. Now, what can be fairer than that?

I shine because I can
and I am

affirmation goddess

Anita Revel

Humility / Vanity

~ I am generous with my light.

~ My beauty is unique, as is that of others.

~ I shine because I can; and because I am who I am.

Humility is one of the seven virtues. It is sometimes described as the reclusive star of the set. This is a curious analogy – when we think of stars we often think of the biggest, shiniest ones that dazzle and impress us... so why would a "reclusive" star be considered virtuous?

The short answer is that the humble star burns only to be charitable with her light. She doesn't look at the bright stars and compare herself. If she did, she may become vain or bitter for there will always be both greater and lesser stars. People who shine in order to gain status and possession are guilty of vanity. Those who shine to make the world a better place, without thought of personal gain or achievement, on the other hand, have the gift of humility.

The ironic thing about humility is, if you think you have it, you don't! Humility means being generous, respectful and gracious without being motivated by gain. Further, these qualities must live in the heart naturally.

Today I am a hugging
and kissing machine

affirmation goddess

Anita Revel

Compassion / Detachment

~ As I love others, I love and care for my Self.
~ I seek to grow closer to my fellow human beings.
~ Having compassion is my key to the inner circle
of humanity.

When loved ones are in pain or distress, a compassionate heart compels you to act in order to relieve them of their suffering. It also compels you to do the same for all of humanity, animals and the environment.

Withholding any form of love – trust, forgiveness, charity, sympathy or even a simple compliment – is withholding an opportunity to grow closer to another human being. If you are unmoved by the mass slaughter of dolphins, by the rampant hunger in third-world countries, or by a work colleague being unfairly sacked, it could mean you are detached from empathy and compassion – the qualities that allow you to share and understand the feelings of others.

The word *compassion* is made up of *co* (together) and *passion* (eagerness), and therefore sets the standard for social behaviour. Giving love to others is giving love to your Self, which in turn lets you enter the inner circle of humanity.

My soul knows how to sing
even when I forget the words

affirmation goddess

Anita Revel

affirmations for creative wellbeing

Speak Your Truth

Productive communication, diplomacy, original work, artistic expression, and truth are all evidence of a healthy state of creative wellbeing. This state gives you the courage to say what needs to be said – constructively, for your highest good, and without the fear of consequence. It is safe to peel away the layers of suppressed truth buried within. You can dig deep for valuable gems that have been forming over time throughout your life and trials.

When you speak your truth you can:

▸ Seek and accept help.
▸ Ask for – and receive – abundance.
▸ Choose your words wisely to get your own way.
▸ Share insights that are precise, astute and relevant.
▸ Manifest abundance in exactly the way you describe.
▸ Aid effective communication between the genders, the young and the old, the experienced and the novice.
▸ Revert to natural and gentle ways of healing rifts and treating injuries.

I'm tasting the fear
and giving it pepper

affirmation goddess

Anita Revel

Assertion / Repression

~ I express my way to happiness!
~ In speaking my truth, I bring my words to life.
~ I assert my desires and they are duly manifested.

No-one likes disharmony, yet most people face some form of it every day. Whether it's internal or going on around you, sometimes it's just easier to give in and shut up than to share how you really feel about a situation.

Ignoring the situation does not make it go away. Repressing your truth converts your self-worth into a bubbling mass of lava that churns and burns your insides and turns you into a stressed-out wreck.

Speaking up might feel like the scarier option in resolving disharmony, but it is the healthiest option for reducing stress levels and clearing the air. It's also the only way to avoid an explosion of lava-ridden words that will change your landscape forever.

It helps to channel repressed feelings into positive, affirmative statements describing your desired outcomes. Even if you choke on the words to start with, asserting your truth is the only cure for subdued honesty and true feelings.

Accepting the truth in myself
lets me accept it in others

affirmation goddess

Anita Revel

Honesty / Denial

~ I speak my truth, act my truth, embody my truth.
~ I am honest in getting to the heart of the matter.
~ There is something "more" and I know what it is.

Sometimes a truth is so deeply buried it's easy to be in denial about it. You know this is the case when you feel queasy, or you become dependent on work, distractions or substances to mask the feeling that, "There must be something more…"

In your heart of hearts, you know when you are lying to your Self, and so does your subconscious and soul.

"Above all else to thine own self be true," wrote William Shakespeare. He knew that life becomes lighter when the truth is revealed. When you are honest, you become less burdened by the effort of keeping the truth hidden. You become more energised when the effort of denial is released and you go to the heart of the matter for resolution.

A healthy throat chakra requires that you pull off your Mask-of-Denial and be absolutely above board, authentic and honest with your Self. Use your intuition, listen to your body and have the courage to act on the messages you hear.

In a world where I can do
anything and be anyone,
I choose to be me and do it well

affirmation goddess

Integrity / Pretence

~ What I think, say and do aligns.

~ I am the good person I appear to be.

~ I enjoy enriching relationships thanks to integrity.

Socrates taught that "The greatest way to live with honour ... is to be what we pretend to be." His lesson promotes the quality of integrity – actually *be*-ing the good person you appear to be, and *do*-ing what is right rather than what is convenient.

Any departure from integrity means you're only pretending. Pretence attracts pretence in equal measure – your reward for insincerity is superficial relationships, artificial luck and a sham reality.

Integrity happens when what you think, say and do all align. With integrity you can fulfil promises because you have the mettle to carry out good intentions. In fact, you only ever make promises you can keep.

You are reliable because of your consistent adherence to being real. And you are trustworthy because you live your truth and honour the truth of others... Strive to be the good person you appear to be.

It's not the size of the
glove in the fight, it's the size
of the love in the glove

affirmation goddess

Anita Revel

Diplomacy / Tactlessness

~ *My words are like arrows – they hit the mark.*
~ *I am Athena personified – diplomatic and true.*
~ *It is truthful and helpful and my timing is perfect .*

Being diplomatic requires patience and discretion. It is being smart with your words; using them wisely to convey truth without injury; and handling negotiations without causing emotional distress. It is beautifully described by Buddha:

If it is not truthful and not helpful, don't say it.

If it is truthful and not helpful, don't say it.

If it is not truthful and helpful, don't say it.

If it is truthful and helpful, wait for the right time.

Sometimes the act of blurting what you know, believe or feel can hurt others. It is important to give careful consideration to the power of your words, and to pause and weigh your words carefully before speaking.

Diplomacy can often require creativity, a gift influenced and enhanced by a healthy throat chakra. If you tend to be tactless, draw on your creative skills to revise and refine your point.

My worries float away
like a bubble on the breeze

affirmation goddess

Anita Revel

Articulation / Incoherence

~ Breathe, breathe, breathe.

~ Pressure begets diamonds; my future is bright!

~ At green traffic lights breathe in; at red lights, out.

There are four types of communication: informational, emotive, persuasive and social. It is important to understand the tone and manner required for each situation, and to be mindful of your speech, body language, facial expression and tone of voice to get your point across effectively.

To aid the clarity of the message, good articulation skills are paramount, using crisp consonants, well-paced delivery and excellent breathing techniques. Yes, even the simple act of breathing can boost your ability to articulate well.

Breathing supplies your body with oxygen, eliminates waste products, and is a fundamental part of articulate speech. Each time you breathe in, feel the spark of energy as the breath is transformed into fuel for your brain and other organs. As you breathe out, be grateful for each breath that purges carbon dioxide from your body.

Keep your breathing regular to boost your clarity and subsequent delivery of your message.

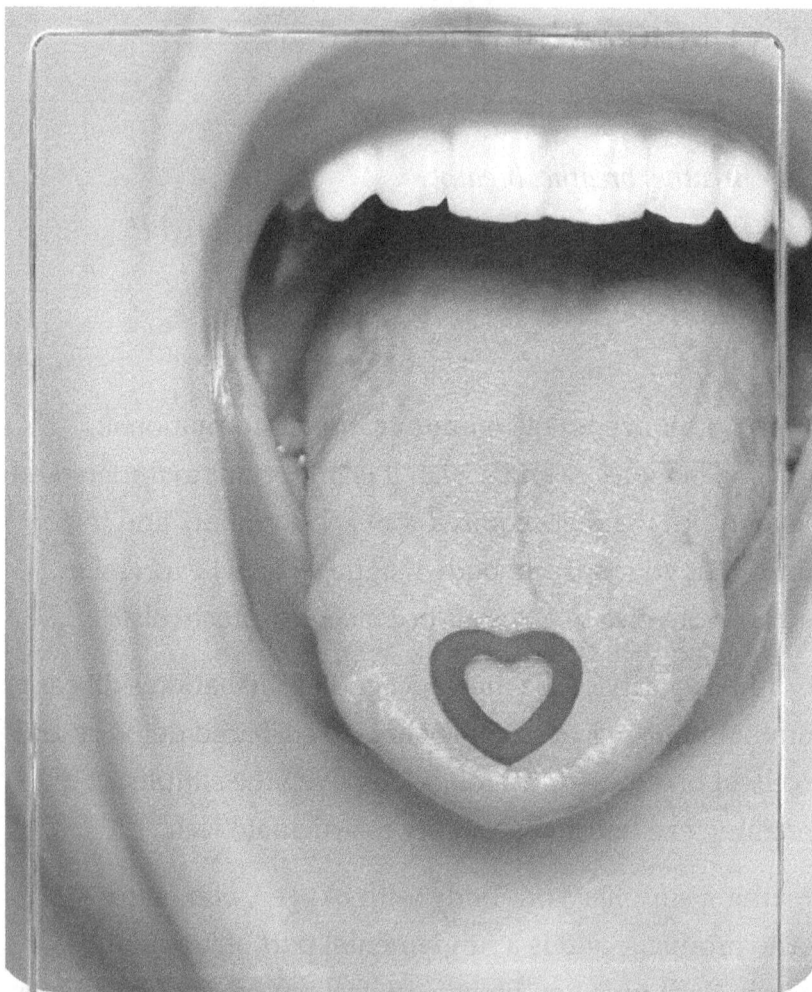

My words have
the power to heal

Healing / Bluntness

~ I am a natural healer and wise woman.
~ What I desire is what I express and manifest.
~ Loving words are always on the tip of my tongue.

Words have the power to hurt as well as to heal. They especially hurt when you gush something you regret later… Pause, and aim to embody the natural healer archetype.

This archetype's shared insights are precise, astute and relevant. When embodying it you are able to seek and accept help, ask for abundance for your highest good, and make your point without aggression.

You can also understand that your expressions manifest in exactly the way you describe. You become adept at aiding effective communication between the genders, the young and the old, the experienced and the novice. When you speak, you are heard. Just as easily, when others speak, you listen.

Above all, the natural healer archetype chooses words wisely to facilitate healing. Your words literally have the power to heal rifts, broken hearts, damaged self-regard and restore healthy self-esteem, both within yourself and others.

My battles are
big enough to care about,
easy enough to win

affirmation goddess

Anita Revel

Resolution / Conflict

> ~ *And so, it is resolved.*
> ~ *It is better to resolve than to resent.*
> ~ *Peaceful resolutions are being achieved for all.*

Incidences of conflict are rife in politics, workplaces, schools and even within families. They may arise when individuals have different ideas about the best course of action, they disagree on moral issues, or one party is expecting the other to read their mind.

Conflict isn't necessarily a bad thing – it helps you debate the merits and pitfalls of the issue at hand. It becomes damaging, however, if a resolution is avoided because you and the other party are afraid of conflict.

You may have been conditioned to be afraid of confrontation because you've been taught to expect rejection or an adverse reaction.

You can condition yourself to be another way, which will help reduce stress levels and promote intimacy and security in your relationships. Do this by staying calm and positive, focusing on a mutually satisfying resolution, and adhering to your true desires for peace.

I relish sunshine,
moonshine and my shine

affirmation goddess

Anita Revel

affirmations for mental wellbeing

See Beauty

You have the power to make the world *outside* your head more beautiful because of what goes on *inside* your head. That is, you can choose to see beauty, both physically and symbolically, simply by deciding to do so. And when you see beauty, you naturally release habits of self-criticism and toxicity. Related to the element of light, seeing beauty helps you feel as *light* as air to drift with the winds of fortune; you can *light* up the stage with your presence; and you can travel *lightly* through life without baggage and regrets.

When you choose to see beauty you can:

▸ Live in a state of clarity.
▸ Readily and easily move on from petty issues.
▸ Make decisions and trust they are right for you.
▸ Simplify your life, both physically and mentally.
▸ See and explore alternative views and viewpoints.
▸ Find solutions by remaining open to divine guidance.
▸ Have regular bursts of epiphany, relish symbolism, and be grateful for the miracles that happen daily.

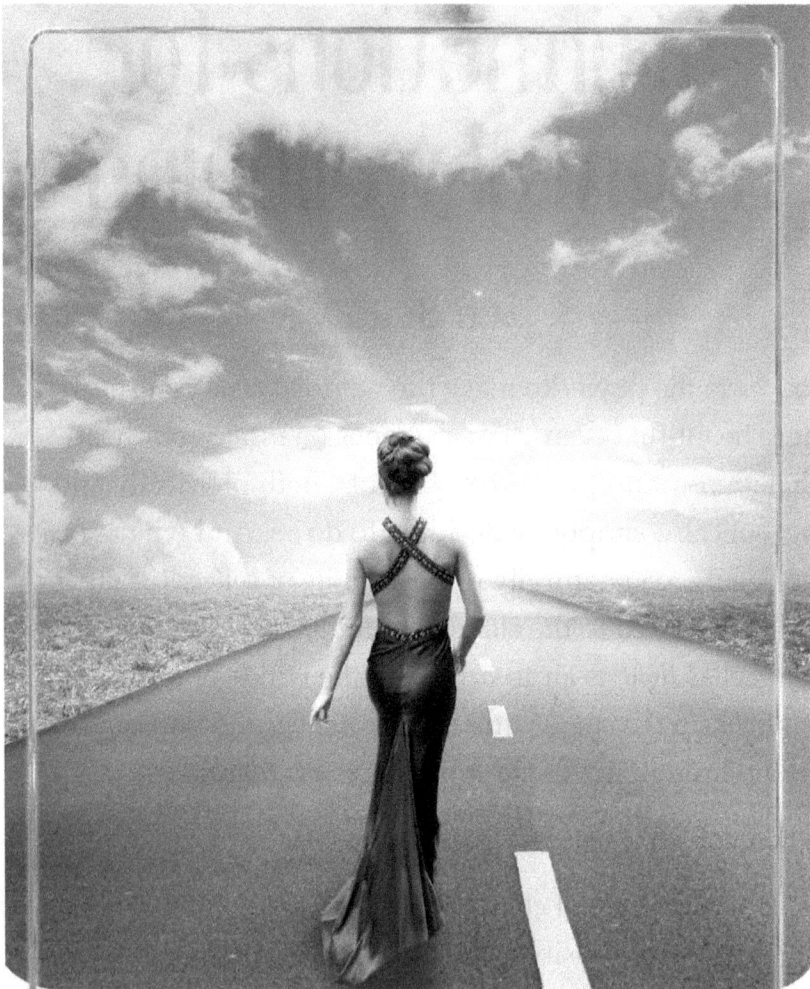

I always take
the right turns at crossroads,
even when they're left ones

affirmation goddess

Anita Revel

Trust / Doubt

> ~ *I was born wise and continue to be so.*
> ~ *The answers that reveal myself to me are correct.*
> ~ *My intuition guides me as to what's right or wrong.*

You were born naturally wise. From your first breath your body guided you to flourish – it told you when to eat, when to drink, when to rest and when to play.

As you grew up, you learned to recognise other signals too – a gut instinct for the right decision; an inner knowing about what's good for you; a sense of right and wrong.

This is your intuition at work; a powerful kind of inner wisdom. It's not necessarily rational or logical, and it's often no more than a hunch or an instinct.

Sadly, many are raised to shut down these messages with a flippant "I'm being silly," or to override the flashes with a derogatory, "I must be crazy."

Release the attachment to toxic thinking that keeps you in a loop of self-doubt. Return to a space of trust for your mental wellbeing. Choose to trust that the answers your intuition reveals to you are correct.

I have wings and
I know how to use them

affirmation goddess

Anita Revel

Reinvention / Stagnancy

~ I give my inner star permission to shine.
~ A fresh future is the mother of reinvention.
~ I am busting loose and launching a new Me.

You are frequently required to be a different person in order to cope with different demands – sometimes you need to be a tigress mother to defend your little ones; at other times you become a butterfly at social events; and on Sunday mornings you can be a sloth lazing until late morning.

It is perfectly natural to marshal energy from different inspiration sources to bring excitement and new gifts to each situation. You can transcend the pitfalls of stagnancy (boredom, decay, self-loathing) by simply refreshing your outlook, renewing your goals and reinventing your Self.

It is time to jump off the sofa and sweep away stagnancy. Paint that picture that is brewing within; enjoy a long, gentle walk along the ocean's shore; paint your toenails a vivid, raunchy red; invite a friend for a shopping expedition and let her talk you into buying daring new clothes…

In other words, it is time to burst free from the constraints of stagnancy, and give your inner star permission to shine.

I am who I am,
I am where I am

affirmation goddess

Anita Revel

Certainty / Procrastination

~ Every decision I make is the right one.

~ I know the what, how and when of my next steps.

~ Taking action is the best way to change my outlook.

There are no lost opportunities; only lost time. With each minute you procrastinate you delay your progress through your evolution. When you delay helping yourself move to the next step, you end up looking at the same old scenery and wondering why things aren't changing for the better.

We're all faced with impossible decisions at times, and maybe procrastination feels safer than the unknown. Whatever your reason for procrastination, decide on a step-by-step action plan that describes what it is you want to achieve, which direction you'd like to take, and how you want each outcome to enrich your life.

Do not get distracted with chit-chat or internet surfing. Do not wander off and begin other tasks. Do not put off until tomorrow what could have been done yesterday.

Trust that each decision you make from intuition and integrity will result in your highest good. Just see yourself enjoying a brighter view at your next stage, and do it!

I am responsible
for what happens next

affirmation goddess

Anita Revel

Care / Indifference

~ I care to care.

~ I strive to know.

~ I am rewarded for my proactiveness.

Any attitude you adopt, whether it be apathy or enthusiasm, is how your brain directs your choices and actions. At an esoteric level, it is energy that the Universe tunes in to. Low frequency energies such as guilt, fear, regret, anger, ignorance or indifference attract low frequency vibes in return. You know you are living in this low vibrational state if you are prone to saying, "I don't know" or "I don't care."

When you care about your life choices and direction, on the other hand, you raise your vibration and the Universe responds with equal gusto. So, pay attention where you're heading, what you're doing and who you're sharing your Self with.

Be conscious of the many small miracles that happen around you every day. Take notice of synchronicity. See symbolism in numbers, visions and happenstance. Increase your awareness of your essence and how it melds or offsets with others. See the clues held within for your spiritual wellbeing. Above all, take responsibility for what happens next.

I have all the time
in the world

affirmation goddess

Anita Revel

Clarity / Clutter

~ *Easy does it.*
~ *I unplug from technology to plug in to life.*
~ *Technology is my friend; Nature is my better friend.*

Technology is supposed to make life streamlined and easier. More often than not though, it speeds it up. It allows you to fit in more communication, more distractions and more chores. The increased activity manifests as energy drain – an endless checklist churned over and over in your head.

You know you are living with a noisy head if you think you can hear the phone ringing (when it's not); you're dependent on hearing "You've got mail!"; the *beep beep* of a text message takes priority over your current task; or your socialising happens primarily via a keyboard and computer screen. If this is you, it means you are expecting too much, doing it too often, working too hard and not relaxing enough.

Embrace the qualities of a serene soul: simplicity, ease and clarity. Turn off computers, schedule phone-free time and spring-clean your space. Promote clarity, practise intuitive wisdom, make *be* your mantra, and set your alarm for Dream O'Clock – a time to relax and enjoy lucid dreaming.

For today at least,
I'm resting on my laurels

affirmation goddess

Anita Revel

Patience / Impatience

~ I am the master of time expansion.
~ Good things come when I am ready.
~ I have plenty of time; all in divine timing.

It's human nature to be inquisitive; to want to turn the page and see what happens next in your story. It becomes a problem, however, when you strive for instant gratification rather than controlling your impulses. Such behaviour leads to long-term failure in life. That is because your attention is on short-term gain rather than the consequences of your impatience.

Yes, you know better than to be impatient, but sometimes you can't help it. You want to get on with what seems to be coming your way. From time to time you may have uttered, "Come on Universe, bring it!" Or the term, "I can't wait!" might be a catch-cry. It is worth remembering that nothing comes until you are ready.

Master the art of time expansion: see yourself having plenty of time to do your next task. Visualise green traffic lights; see deadlines as *alive*-lines; and imagine yourself taking a break – even if it's just for one day at a time, initially.

I trust in my Self;
not in the Self I think I should be,
but in the goddess that I am

affirmation goddess

Anita Revel

Light / Darkness

~ *Let there be light!*

~ *It is still a beautiful world.*

~ *My present is light, bright and outasight!*

On the first day, God said, "Let there be light." As such, light was the first element in the creation of humanity. It follows then that illumination, both physically and philosophically, is integral to your psyche.

Typically, to be in the dark is to feel isolated and confused, yet not all darkness is bad. The yin yang shows us this.

Darkness, like light, is energy from the original source and therefore sacred. Resting under the shade of a tree in summer, hibernating in winter, even floating inside the warm darkness of the womb… these moments of darkness are natural balancers so that you may recognise light when it is time. Darkness only becomes negative when it spirals into self-sabotage, self-criticism and excessive introspection. At such times, heed the words of Desiderata:

With all its sham drudgery and broken dreams,
it is still a beautiful world.

Today my spirit
is swanning in paradise

affirmation goddess

Anita Revel

affirmations for spiritual wellbeing

Understand Bliss

Spiritual wellbeing facilitates your connection with your faith system. When in this state, you can know what it is to be at peace. Self-knowledge and pure awareness is awakened, and your many forms of knowledge are activated – cognitive, emotional, intuitive, learned, to name a few. In short, you will effortlessly be able to understand bliss.

When you know, understand and experience bliss, you can:

▸ Know your calling and honour your destiny.

▸ Interpret messages from Mother Earth via symbols.

▸ Understand and experience bliss, even if only for one moment each day.

▸ Be a cosmic traveller, time expander and sacred vessel for divine expression.

▸ Intuitively and effortlessly share your gifts of wisdom, understanding and spiritual knowledge.

▸ See yourself as a minute organism in the ways of the world, both in the physical and non-physical planes, in the present and the future.

Though my path may twist
and skew, all the better for
an awesome view

affirmation goddess

Anita Revel

Bliss / Gloom

~ Blessings abound.

~ This lesson is preparing me to bloom.

~ I count my blissings, and count myself lucky.

The chrysanthemum is a plant that flourishes more freely if it is pinched back in spring – this is the process whereby the growing shoots are slightly damaged in order to promote more vigorous growth outwards.

It is an interesting analogy to your own life. Providing you see each obstacle as a lesson rather than a hindrance, you can grow naturally stronger with each adversity.

It is completely OK to hibernate in a cave while you rejuvenate, but follow this period of introspection with lots of healing laughter to surmount the gloom.

This little ditty will help you remember your priorities when looking on the bright side:

Count your wins instead of your woes;

Count your blissings instead of your blows;

Count your friends instead of your foes;

Count yourself lucky to counteract sorrows.

Half of being wise
is knowing when to learn

affirmation goddess

Anita Revel

Wisdom / Ignorance

~ I am learning and growing every single day.
~ I know I don't know but I know I can change that.
~ I operate partly from right-brain space, partly from left-brain space, and 100 percent from heart space.

There are many kinds of knowledge: cognitive, intuitive, intellectual, spiritual, creative and emotional. Each form is energised differently – business acumen is ruled by the left-brain, for example, whereas spiritual and creative wisdom belongs more to the right-brain realm.

You were born with your own style of innate wisdom which continues to grow every day. Whether your knowledge comes from listening to others, reading books, watching how it's done, or rolling up your sleeves and doing it by trial and error, strive to remain open to learning something new every day to avoid becoming stale and ignorant.

Sure, you might not always know the best way forward, but it's better to do something than to linger in ignorance. There's no shame in not knowing something. Just knowing that you can learn is enough. After all, half of being wise is knowing that you can, and will, always continue to learn.

I can reframe my reality
whenever I choose

affirmation goddess

Anita Revel

Gratitude / Blame

> ~ I am grateful for this lesson.
> ~ Thank you legs for helping me move on and dance!
> ~ I am thankful for the little blessings that present
>   themselves to me hundreds of times a day.

When you live with gratitude, taking notice of the thousands of daily blessings becomes your focus and takes priority over hardships, hurts and blame. When you blame others for their transgressions (or problems in general), you are keeping that sad situation in focus. Staying in this negative loop also acts as a metaphorical crutch, so you limp through life blaming others instead of accepting responsibility and moving on.

When your attention is on gratitude for a warm bed, hot food, laughing children, good friends and even running water, you are charging your Self with positive power. Be grateful for every little miracle and feel yourself becoming super-charged.

Throw away the crutch crafted with blame and resentment. Instead of saying, "I blame you..." reframe your thinking to: "I am grateful for this lesson." Feel how this new attitude creates a world shift for your outlook and peace of mind.

Peace of mind begins
with a piece of heart

affirmation goddess

Anita Revel

Peace of Mind / Hardship

~ *This too, shall pass.*

~ *Pressure begets diamonds.*

~ *With rain comes rainbows; with darkness, the stars.*

American abolitionist and social reformer Henry Ward Beecher wrote, "Affliction comes to us, not to make us sad but sober; not to make us sorry but wise."

It's true. Unless we have rain we don't get rainbows; without darkness we can't see the stars; and without long-term pressure we don't get diamonds.

Hardship may make you uncomfortable and unsettled, but it acts as a benchmark of what unhappiness (and therefore happiness) feels like. That is, in knowing hardship you can look forward to the sacred and natural balancer – a corresponding degree of happiness.

Liken any hardship you experience to the swing of a pendulum, which arcs in equal measure from one height to another. It doesn't swing to halfway then return to its origin – it completes the natural cycle of high/low/high. Recite, "This too, will pass," and enjoy the upswing of the pendulum's return.

No matter the depths
to which I dive,
the view confirms I am alive

affirmation goddess

Anita Revel

Transcendence / Depression

~ Watch me fly!
~ Upwards I rise, reborn and wise.
~ Onwards and upwards, ever I fly;
  with grace and good fortune as my alibi.

Transcendence is a great tool for dealing with daily, boring monotony. It's not so much about separating yourself from the messy side of life and denying it's there, as it is about rising above the muck with grace.

Accepting the muck, and staying in it, is the same as accepting inertia, and eventually depression.

Invoke your capacity for compassion in order to learn tolerance for your Self and the various mood-changes you travel through. When you can be gentle with your Self, you are better able to see yourself being accepted by your circle in all your phases.

Suddenly you will feel less isolated and more understood. In turn, it will be a breeze to transcend the stagnancy and the blues. Your energy will increase, your mood will elevate, and it will be easier to accept that these challenges are here to make you stronger – that you can suffer without suffering.

Today I am smiling
for no reason

affirmation goddess

Anita Revel

Positive Thoughts / Toxicity

~ Happy thoughts, happy life.
~ I change my mind to change my mind.
~ I think, therefore hope, for the best at all times.

The crucial element that separates humans from other creatures is the ability to think independently, logically and constructively. So why, when endowed with such beautiful abilities, do humans succumb to toxicity?

Toxic thoughts and self-limiting beliefs crush your spirit. Your connection with the outside world is shut down while you wallow in self-pity and sabotage. Life becomes difficult, and you doubt your value as your self-esteem unravels.

It helps to visualise a red stop sign when such toxicity occurs, and consciously snap yourself back into a positive mindset. Reprogramming your brain to think positively is the only way of cancelling out toxic noise. To think and behave otherwise is not only toxic, but wasteful of your gifts.

Whether you take advantage of your ability to think positively or squander it, you are subject to the relevant consequences. So change your mind to change your mind and think for the best.

Angel blessings all around;
love and light does abound

affirmation goddess

Anita Revel

Child of the Universe / Empty Vessel

~ I have consent to feel deserving.
~ Angels are carrying me on their wings.
~ I am a divine being having a divine experience.

You are a child of the Universe. You came into this world as a perfect being. You are heaven sent and the embodiment of innocence and perfection. It is a celebration of your origins and your destiny to reconnect with your perfect Self – the innocent, joyful child within.

American businesswoman Mary Kay Ash once said, "Aerodynamically the bumblebee shouldn't be able to fly, but the bumblebee doesn't know that so it goes on flying anyway." Likewise, return to your childhood innocence and soar above any perceived limitations, even if you think you can't!

No matter what your faith system, know that you are supported in your efforts, providing they're for the greatest good of all. Have the courage to go where angels fear to tread, for if they are not treading there, they are simply carrying you on their wings. And, know that you are a human being having a divine experience, *and* a divine being having a human experience.

What I desire is
what I manifest

affirmation goddess

affirmations for holistic wellbeing

Be In a Perfect State of Love and Trust

On a metaphysical level, you balance your chakras to assist in energy flow throughout your body. On physical, spiritual, psychological and emotional levels, striving for the best in each of the seven states of wellbeing brings you an overall sense of calm and contentment. You can enjoy peace of mind, and a sense that all is well in your world. When your seven major chakras are in flow and the seven states of wellbeing are in order, so is your life. It becomes easy to *be* in a perfect state of love and trust.

You know you are in a perfect state of love and trust when:

- The purpose of your life becomes apparent.
- It is effortless to balance work, home and social lives.
- You can manifest exactly what you ask for and deserve.
- You become naturally magnetic to equally beautiful people and happenings.
- Inspiring others becomes an organic extension of what you already do rather than something you work at.

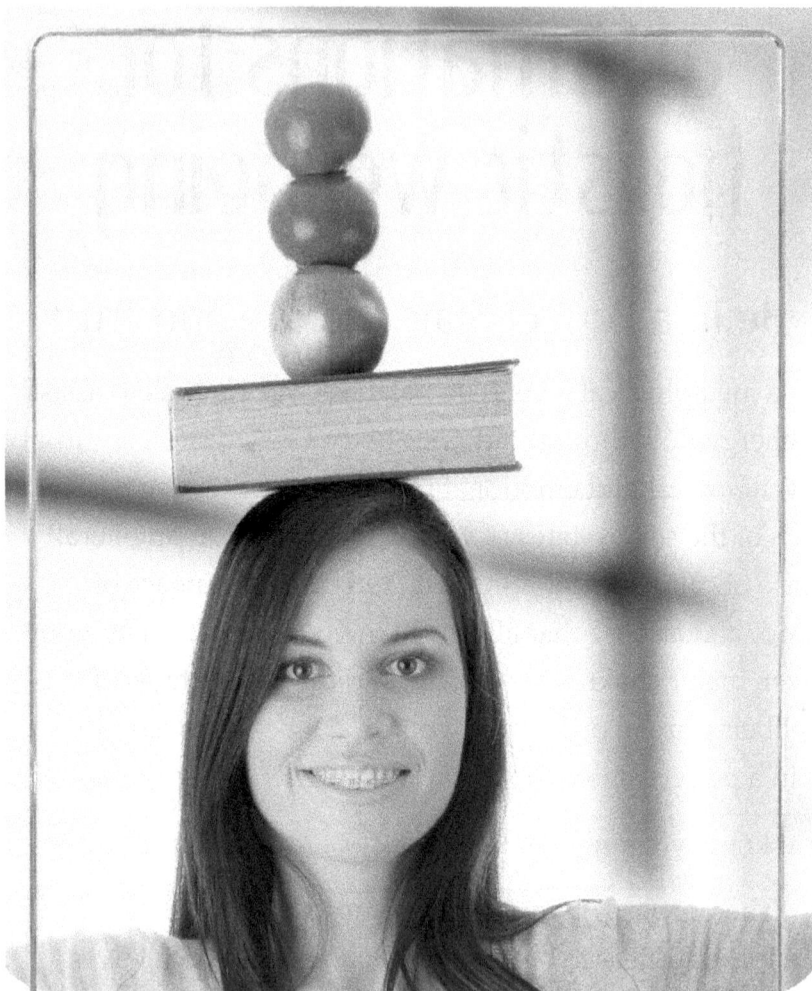

My physical and spiritual worlds
are in perfect harmony

affirmation goddess

Anita Revel

Balance / Disparity

~ *I am a divine being enjoying my physical world.*

~ *I balance my roles and my time with perfect poise.*

~ *Work, home and play balance is absolutely doable.*

The noblest act of self-respect is to strive for balance between the physical and the spiritual to foster healthy energy flow through your chakras. Balancing your chakras balances your very being, ergo your life. And focusing on each of the states of wellbeing lets you strike the chord that brings harmony to every aspect of your work, home and play lives.

There is no need to meditate 24/7 under a crystal pyramid to become enlightened; nor do you need to become a barefoot vegetarian to be grounded. By simply willing it, your base chakra can stretch and grow like tree roots into Mother Earth to thrive on her delicious grounding energy; while your crown chakra can shine its rainbow light to draw on the Universe's uplifting spiritual energy.

In keeping consciousness in both worlds, your body can stretch, yawn and wake up to the electric knowing that a divine being can be happy in a physical world, and vice versa. Work, home and play balance becomes doable!

Round and round and round
she goes, the world revolves
around she who glows

affirmation goddess

True Beauty / Superficiality

> ~ *I am beautiful to the core.*
> ~ *My beauty is in my rainbow light.*
> ~ *My true beauty shines from every pore.*

Ideals of outer beauty vary between cultures, genders and age groups, but there is one principle that no-one can deny is true: outer beauty fades, inner beauty is forever.

If you've ever cut open a shiny red apple to find a rotten core, you can see that outer beauty is meaningless without a ripe, juicy centre to complete the package. It is disappointing to find a rotten core, or a rotten personality, because a beautiful promise has been betrayed.

True beauty is when your personality has a tangible effect on your external appearance – laugh lines, soft eyes, a warm glow. True beauty is when all seven chakras are in alignment and energy is flowing beautifully through your auric body. And true beauty is when your inner rainbow manifests as an irresistible glow.

Ultimately, as a truly beautiful person, you can become a magnet to similarly beautiful things, happenings and beings in your life.

Healthy body, healthy mind,
enlightened spirit is intertwined

affirmation goddess

Anita Revel

Peace / Stress

~ I am at peace.

~ Peace begins with me.

~ I am completely at ease as a divine, physical and emotional being.

To wish you'd done things differently, that you had taken more risks and opportunities, is not simply regretting your past; it's regretting your present too.

Likewise, to be always planning for the future, or fearing there is not enough time, is also regretting your present.

It is time to return to your Self now. For this moment at least, feel what it is like to be sitting in the palm of God and in the heart of Goddess. Right this minute, for as long as you need to be here, choose peace of mind. Be quiet within your body, which is your physical manifestation of your inner beauty. Also be at peace with your faith, whatever you conceive your faith system to be.

Peace of mind is connecting these three crucial relationships between body, mind and spirit. And so, for the time being, connect the dots and become completely at ease in your divine, physical and emotional embodiment.

with gratitude...

Thank you so much to the many co-travellers who have shaped my experiences, helped me grow and intensified my joys. I am deeply grateful for your lessons and your advice, and to have you beside me in this most wonderful journey we call *life*. Blissed be! ♥ Anita

about the author

Anita Revel is a creatrix, author, mother and wife, web diva, dream weaver and lover of life. She's also a teacher, artist, traveller and joy junkie but couldn't make these rhyme. Nevertheless, these roles pretty well sum up her passion for inspired living.

Anita is the creator of an ever-growing collection of well-being resources at igoddess.com, a columnist for United Press International, and the author of numerous books for women's wellbeing.

Anita is also a Civil Marriage Celebrant in her home region of Margaret River in Western Australia – one of the most beautiful wine producing regions in the world. She lives on a farm with her husband, daughter and a dog as loyal as his nearest cuddle, but travels the world offering workshops and weddings!

Keep up to date with Anita's work via AnitaRevel.com.

also by anita revel

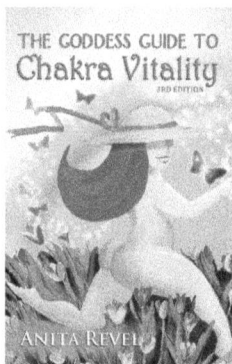

The Goddess Guide to Chakra Vitality, 3rd edition

This ever-popular handbook contains many easy ways to sass up your chakras – the energy centres that rule every aspect of your life. It outlines tools such as sound, elements, symbols, colours, flowers, gemstones, essential oils, movement, visualisations, affirmations and goddess power to help bring balance into your life.

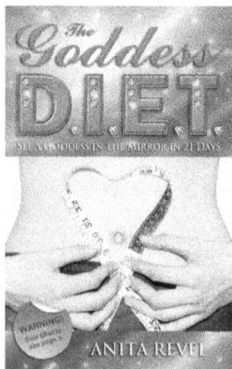

ISBN 9 780980 6061 8 8
94 pages, AUD $19.95

The Goddess DIET, See a Goddess in the Mirror in 21 Days

No more dangerous dieting; no more trash talking; no more self-loathing… This book outlines dozens of Daily Intentional Empowerment Tools to realign physical, emotional and spiritual behaviours for holistic wellbeing. In 21 days you can lose your inner critic, gain more energy and fall in self-love.

ISBN 9 780980 4439 1 2
256 pages, AUD $24.95

BOTIBOTO, Beautiful On The Inside, Beautiful On The Outside; An Empowerment Story for Well-Rounded Women

BOTIBOTO is a modern tale of celebrities, body image, and how one girl found her divine inner spark because of it all. Beautifully illustrated by Sally Grant.

ISBN 9 780980 4439 3 6
33 pages, AUD $24.95

7 Day Bootcamp for Brides – Feel Fit, Focused and Fabulous on Your Wedding Day

Embrace your awesomeness in just seven days. Stick with the program and keep your gorgeous glow for the rest of your life! This program was developed by fitness coaches, nutritionists and motivational experts, so you can be sure it's the most practical and safe program for you as the bride-to-be.

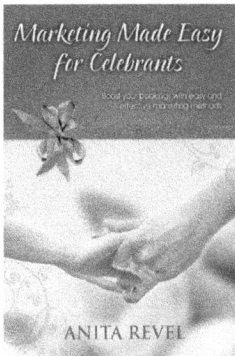

ISBN 9 780980 4439 7 4
102 pages, US $14.95

Marketing Made Easy for Celebrants – Boost Your Bookings with Easy and Effective Marketing Methods

This step-by-step guide will help you craft marketing strategies at low cost and low risk. With the worksheets and templates included in this book, you can create and action your own marketing plan within minutes. Watch your celebrancy business grow with every strategy you put into place.

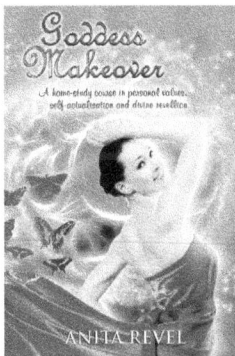

ISBN 9 780980 4439 6 7
116 pages, AUD $34.95

Goddess Makeover, A Home-Study Course in Personal Values, Self-Actualisation and Divine Revellion

This home-study course is perfect for every woman seeking to live more consciously within her Self, her soul and her community. To learn the seven rules of a self-actualised goddess you will create a Values Totem, and in the process, reveal your personal value system that defines your goddess within.

ISBN 9 780557 2842 7 6
104 pages, US $14.95

www.ingramcontent.com/pod-product-compliance
Lightning Source LLC
Chambersburg PA
CBHW072124090426
42739CB00012B/3056